Persephone

Contents

The Gods of Ancient Greece *Profiles and pronunciation guide*	2
The Story of Persephone *A story from Greek mythology*	4
The Seasons *A poem*	23
Summer, Autumn, Winter, Spring *A scrapbook*	24
Why Do the Seasons Change? *An explanation*	28
The Persephone Debate *A debate and instructions*	30
Think and Link *Questions to discuss*	32

The Gods of

In ancient times, stories of gods were told.

Aphrodite
(say *a-fruh-**digh**-tee*)
Goddess of love and beauty

Roman name: Venus

Apollo
(say *a-**pol**-loh*)
God of light, healing, music, prophecy and poetry

Roman name: Apollo

Ares
(say ***air**-reez*)
God of war

Roman name: Mars

Hades
(say ***hay**-deez*)
God of the Underworld

Roman name: Pluto

Hera
(say ***heer**-uh*)
Goddess of marriage

Roman name: Juno

Hermes
(say ***hur**-meez*)
Messenger of the gods

Roman name: Mercury

Ancient Greece

Read about some, then Persephone's tale will unfold.

Athena
(say *a-**thee**-nuh*)
Goddess of crafts, war and wisdom

Roman name: Minerva

Demeter
(say *duh-**mee**-tuh*)
Goddess of plants and crops

Roman name: Ceres

Eros
(say ***eer**-ros*)
God of love

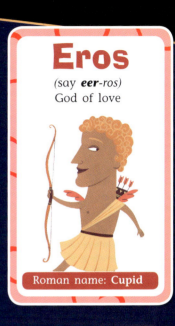

Roman name: Cupid

Persephone
(say *pur-**sef**-uh-nee*)
Daughter of Demeter and Zeus

Roman name: Proserpina

Poseidon
(say *puh-**sigh**-din*)
God of water and the sea

Roman name: Neptune

Zeus
(say ***zyews***)
Ruler of the gods

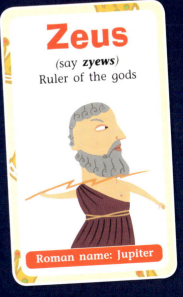

Roman name: Jupiter

The Story of Persephone

Long ago, a goddess named Persephone was wandering in the lush rolling hills with her friends. The sun smiled upon the young women as they picked armfuls of sweet-smelling flowers.

Persephone's mother, Demeter, goddess of plants and crops, kept watch nearby.

But she was not the only one watching her daughter. Persephone was being spied upon by Hades, King of the Underworld. The Underworld was a shadowy place beneath the earth where people's spirits lived on after they died.

Hades had fallen in love with the beautiful young Persephone. He used his powers to have a narcissus—a slender, pearly flower—planted in her path.

As Persephone bent to touch its stem, the ground before her split open like a ripe peach. Hades burst out of the earth in his golden chariot and seized the young goddess. Before Persephone could cry for help, Hades' coal-black horses had swiftly pulled his chariot back down to the Underworld.

This happened so quickly that Demeter did not even see Hades or his chariot. She searched all over the hillside for her daughter, calling and sobbing, but could not find her.

Demeter was so saddened by Persephone's disappearance that she could not be comforted. She could not carry out her duties as goddess of plants and crops, and all over the land, flowers began to droop and harvests failed.

Deep in the shadows of the Underworld, Hades told Persephone of his great love for her. "I have brought you here," he said softly to her, "to be my wife."

Persephone wept, broken-hearted. "I miss my mother—as well as the sunny hillside where I used to laugh with my friends." But she had no choice but to stay with Hades in the Underworld.

Above the ground, Demeter continued her determined search for Persephone. She journeyed far and wide. "Have you seen my lovely daughter?" she asked everyone she met. No one had.

As Demeter searched, her sadness grew. The land became dry and hard, the flowers withered and the green leaves sickened and died. Even the air grew chill, turning the blue sky to grey. People went hungry because their crops did not ripen.

Finally, after many months had passed, Demeter discovered what had happened to Persephone.

In a rage, she flew to the home of Zeus, Persephone's father and King of the Gods.

"Persephone must be returned to me at once," she demanded.

Zeus wanted to please Demeter. He also knew that his kingdom had suffered because of her loss.

"Persephone can return to you," he told Demeter, "but she may stay above ground only if she has eaten nothing from the Underworld."

Zeus sent a speedy messenger named Hermes to fetch his daughter. But now Persephone could not decide what to do. While she longed to see her mother, she had grown fond of Hades during her time underground and had become his wife. She enjoyed welcoming spirits to the Underworld as their Queen.

Hades was happy for Persephone to visit her mother, but he wanted his wife to return to him and their underground kingdom.

"Here is some food for your journey," he said. He held out a ripe, juicy pomegranate.

The juice left a red stain on Persephone's lips.

When Demeter saw Persephone, she embraced her daughter and laughed with joy. Demeter's laughter warmed the land, bringing forth shoots and buds. Trees sprouted lacy green shawls, and the tall feathery grasses danced once again upon the hillsides.

Vine tendrils and ferns unfurled their tender tips. Flowers cascaded where the land had been bare and blighted. Animals and birds crept out from their quiet resting places into a world of sunshine.

But Zeus saw at once from her reddened lips that Persephone had eaten some pomegranate seeds. He said to her, "You have eaten food from Hades' kingdom, therefore you must go back to the Underworld."

Persephone wept at the thought of leaving her mother again, but at the same time, she was happy to return to her husband.

From that time on, Persephone spent half the year on earth with her mother and the other half in the Underworld with Hades.

And so every year, the story tells, Demeter mourns the loss of her daughter and the land turns chill and grey. But when Persephone returns to her mother, the land—like Demeter—celebrates the end of winter and the coming of spring.

The Seasons

Spring is tender green
Blossoms celebrate the sun
Nature wakes again.

Summer brings blue skies
Beaming sun on sandy shores
Corn must ripen soon.

Autumn is red-hued
Pumpkins shine on straggly vines
Leaves are falling fast.

Winter's sombre shades
Grey and white with dark-barked trees
Nature rests again.

Summer, Autumn,

The seasons change as the year goes by. Here's a scrapbook—from a photographer's eye.

Summer time! The sun is shining and the living is easy. Birds are singing, bees are buzzing and the fragrance of flowers fills the warm air. Green leaves take in sunlight and fruit hangs on the vine for picking.

A grasshopper eats wild flower petals. It looks like a leaf to fool its predators.

A rosehip is the fruit of the wild rose. It ripens when the rose petals fall.

People and animals like to eat chestnuts. The sweet nuts grow in a spiky coat.

Wild flowers look beautiful. To insects, they taste good, too!

Winter, Spring

Autumn brings a kaleidoscope of colours. There's magic in the air, together with the cool winds of change. It's time to harvest crops and the last of nature's wild bounties.

Animals such as the squirrel collect and store food for the cold months ahead.

Some seeds are blown away by the wind, to find new places to grow.

Mushrooms grow in damp earth that is still warm from summer.

Some leaves change colour in the cooler months. Green changes to orange and brown.

Winter has the earth in its grip. Cold landscapes seem still and quiet. Plants and animals slow down and save their energy for spring. In some places, water freezes into ice, and snow blankets the ground.

Leaves fall on a frozen pond. Beneath the surface, animals and plants wait for spring.

A songbird stays within winter's reach, eating seeds, hips and berries.

Wild birds take off on the last leg of their migration to warmer grounds.

Day breaks over a wintry wetland. The sun shines but does not warm the cold earth.

Spring unfolds with wet and warmer days. The fresh smells of plants emerge from the earth. As the sun warms the earth, there are bird songs and choruses of peeping frogs. The cycle of life continues.

A songbird welcomes spring with song. It seeks a mate and a new home.

A salamander emerges from the cold pond and basks in the warm sun.

Wild flowers start to bloom in spring's warm showers and longer days.

Mint plants flaunt their lush green growth sparked by energy from the sun.

The Earth moves (like a spinning top) around the sun. Look how the seasons change, one by one.

Why Do the Seasons Change?

THE SEASONS CHANGE as the Earth moves around (or orbits) the sun. The Earth is like a spinning top, tipped slightly to one side. It is this tilt (23°) that causes the seasons to change.

As the Earth travels around the sun, it remains tilted in the same direction. This means that sometimes one half of the Earth (or hemisphere) is tilted towards the sun, and sometimes it is tilted away.

- The hemisphere tilted towards the sun absorbs more of the sun's heat, so the weather is warmer.
- The hemisphere tilted away from the sun absorbs less of the sun's heat, so the weather is cooler.

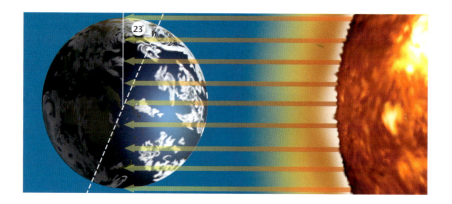

NORTHERN HEMISPHERE

The northern hemisphere is tilted towards the sun. Days are longer and nights are shorter.

❶ SUMMER SOLSTICE
about 21 June

Both hemispheres receive the same amount of sunlight. Days and nights are roughly equal in length.

❷ SPRING EQUINOX
about 21 March

❹ AUTUMN EQUINOX
about 22 September

The northern hemisphere is tilted away from the sun. Days are shorter and nights are longer.

❸ WINTER SOLSTICE
about 21 December

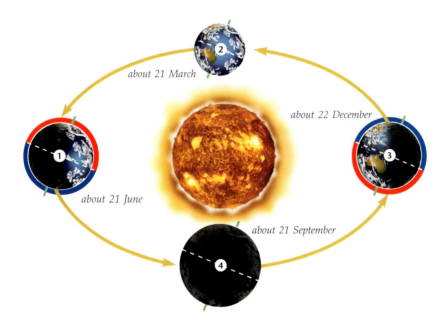

❶ WINTER SOLSTICE
about 21 June

The southern hemisphere is tilted away from the sun. Days are shorter and nights are longer.

❷ AUTUMN EQUINOX
about 21 March

❹ SPRING EQUINOX
about 22 September

Both hemispheres receive the same amount of sunlight. Days and nights are roughly equal in length.

❸ SUMMER SOLSTICE
about 21 December

The southern hemisphere is tilted towards the sun. Days are longer and nights are shorter.

SOUTHERN HEMISPHERE

The Persephone Debate

If Hades and Demeter had a debate, what would have been Persephone's fate?

Topic: That Persephone should stay with Hades in the Underworld.

Proponent: Hades

Opposition: Demeter

Opening statement

I believe that Persephone should stay with me. She is my beloved wife and her job is to welcome spirits to the Underworld. If she visits her mother, she may never return and I will become very sad and grumpy.

Questions that I could ask Demeter

- Why didn't she look after her daughter more carefully in the first place?
- Why isn't she doing her work on earth properly?

Answers to questions that Demeter may ask me

- The Underworld is a wonderful place. It's not gloomy everywhere!
- I do not want to live above the earth. I'm happy in the Underworld.

Opening statement

I believe that Persephone should not stay in the Underworld. She is my beloved daughter and when she is gone, I am too sad to look after the land properly. Hades kidnapped her! That's a crime. He should be punished by giving up his wife.

Questions that I could ask Hades

- Who would want to live in the dark, gloomy Underworld?
- Why didn't he find a wife by dating girls rather than kidnapping one?

Answers to questions that Hades may ask me

- I don't want to live with my married daughter. That can cause trouble!
- No, doing more exercise and buying new clothes won't cheer me up.

Think and Link

Poem and Scrapbook
How is the language similar in these texts? How is it different?

Profiles and Story
How do the character profiles help you to read and understand the story? Do you think it is important to pronounce words correctly? Why?

Making Inferences
How do you use your personal experience of:
- family relationships
- the changing seasons

to help you understand the myth?

Explanation and Debate
Which text presents information in an objective and balanced way? How does the language tell you that the text is based on science?

Which text presents personal opinions? How is the language different?

Scrapbook and Explanation
Which of these texts gives a personal view of the seasons? Why?

How does the language differ in these texts? How do these texts differ visually?

Pictures of the Seasons
Which picture of winter would you like to write about? Which picture of summer? Why?